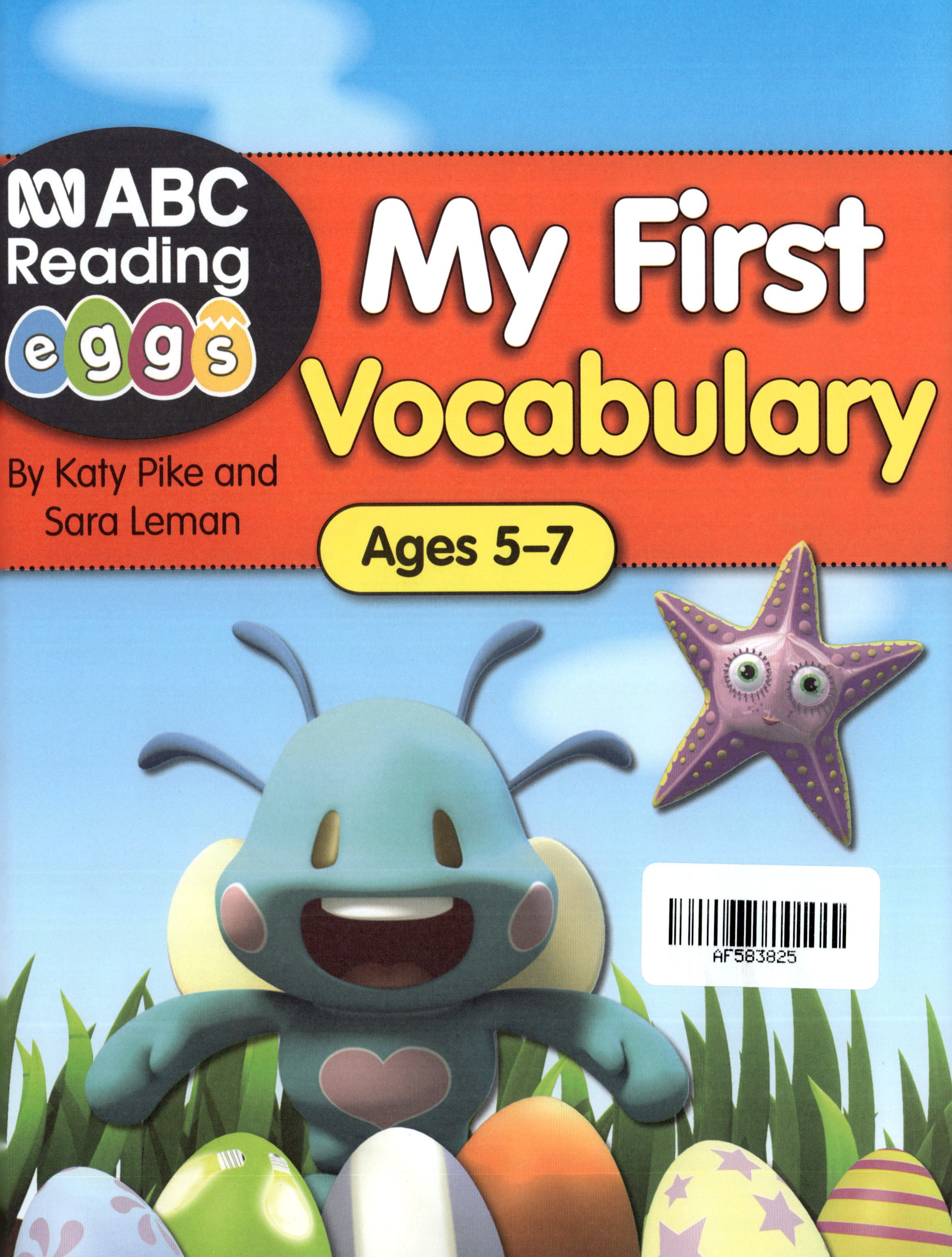
ABC Reading eggs
My First Vocabulary
By Katy Pike and Sara Leman
Ages 5–7

ABC Reading eggs

Dear Parent or Carer,

This book is part of the **My First** series of **Reading Eggs** workbooks. **Reading Eggs** has proven to be very popular with parents, children and teachers. The **Reading Eggs** books and website have helped more than 20 million children worldwide learn to read.

Each vibrant book in the **My First** series includes a wide range of interesting activities that will help your child develop essential reading and writing skills. Written by experienced teachers and educators, the series supports what your child learns at school.

The pages are clear and uncluttered, with activities that build real skills. Activities are fun and motivate children to continue working and learning. Instructions are easy to follow and regular challenges entice children to extend their learning.

I hope that you and your child enjoy using this and other books in the series.

Kind regards, Katy Pike
Publisher

ABC Reading Eggs My First Vocabulary

ISBN: 978-1-74215-171-7

Reprinted 2011, 2015, 2017, 2020, 2025

Distributed by:
Pascal Press
PO Box 250
Glebe NSW 2037

www.readingeggs.com
Written by Katy Pike and Sara Leman
Publisher: Katy Pike
Editors: Amanda Santamaria and Stacey Weston
Design and layout by Modern Art Production Group
Printed China by 1010 Printing International Ltd

Contents

Activities 4 – 5
In the family 6 – 9
All sorts of shapes 10 – 13
At home 14 – 17
Playtime 18 – 21
In the picture 1 22 – 23
Down on the farm 24 – 27
At the shops 28 – 31
3D objects 32 – 35
Tick tock 36 – 39
In the picture 2 40 – 41
Party time 42 – 45
Moving around 46 – 49
Ahoy me hearties 50 – 53
People who help us 54 – 57
In the picture 3 58 – 59
Ordinal numbers 60 – 63
At the restaurant 64 – 67
Seasonal things 68 – 71
Things to wear 72 – 75
In the picture 4 76 – 77
Revision 78 – 79
Certificate 80

Vocabulary activities to do at home

Building vocabulary is an essential skill. Not only does vocabulary help children to communicate effectively, it also enhances reading comprehension.

You can help your child to enhance their vocabulary simply through conversation with them. Include new words and if necessary, make sure that you provide a simple definition that your child will understand. Encourage your child to use the new words in further conversations.

Sorting and classifying things are useful skills. Allow your child to look through old magazines and to cut out pictures that appeal to them. Ask them if they can name each image and if they can find some way of sorting these images into groups. Can they provide a name for each group of things? What do these groups have in common? How are they different?

Reading with your child is an excellent way of introducing new words into their vocabulary. If your child encounters an unfamiliar word briefly define it in simple terms and if possible, provide a further example of how this word might be used.

Encouraging your child to read a wide variety of texts will develop their vocabulary. Be ready to help your child with definitions if necessary. A children's picture dictionary can be very helpful in assisting with

definitions and vocabulary building. The local library is also a great source of books that will introduce your child to a range of texts.

Encourage your child to help you in a variety of situations that involve 'technical' vocabulary. For example allowing your child to assist you in the kitchen introduces them to interesting words such as 'steaming', 'scrambling', 'poaching', 'spatula' and 'colander'. Following a recipe together with your child can also introduce them to a variety of mathematical terms such as 'millilitre', 'litre', 'grams', and 'kilograms'.

Labelling things can be a helpful way to encourage your child to learn new words. Start with a room in the house and label each object with a sticky note. Encourage your child to help you and together study the names on each label. Leave the labels there for a while and refer to them regularly. Detach the labels and then ask your child to see if they can stick the labels back on the correct objects. Provide your child with plenty of praise and encouragement.

Children learn new skills more effectively when they are motivated. Therefore it is important to make vocabulary learning fun and not a chore. Try acting out a word and asking your child to tell you what the word is. Alternatively you could provide your child with a word and ask them to draw it.

Playing games such as 'I went to market and bought some pawpaws, a pineapple and some lychees...', telling jokes and making up rhymes are great ways to enhance vocabulary. On car journeys, try pointing to an object or telling your child a word and then asking them to give you a rhyming word. Young children will often make up nonsense rhymes but this is OK. They are simply having fun exploring and playing with language.

Lesson 1 • In the family

All families are different.

1 Draw a line from the person to the word.

mother daughter grandmother

son father

2 Match up the pairs.

sister

father

aunt

grandfather

mother

brother

grandmother

uncle

3 Join each person to a label.

mum

sister

dad

brother

grandma

grandpa

4 Choose the best word to complete each sentence.

grandparents cousins sister aunty

My ______________ is annoying.

Our ______________ come to see us when we have a party.

My uncle is married to my ______________.

These are my ______________.

5 **Label this family. Use these words, mother, father, son, daughter, grandmother, grandfather.**

CHALLENGE

Draw and label your own family.
Can you be both a sister and a daughter?
Yes or No.

Unit 2 • All sorts of shapes

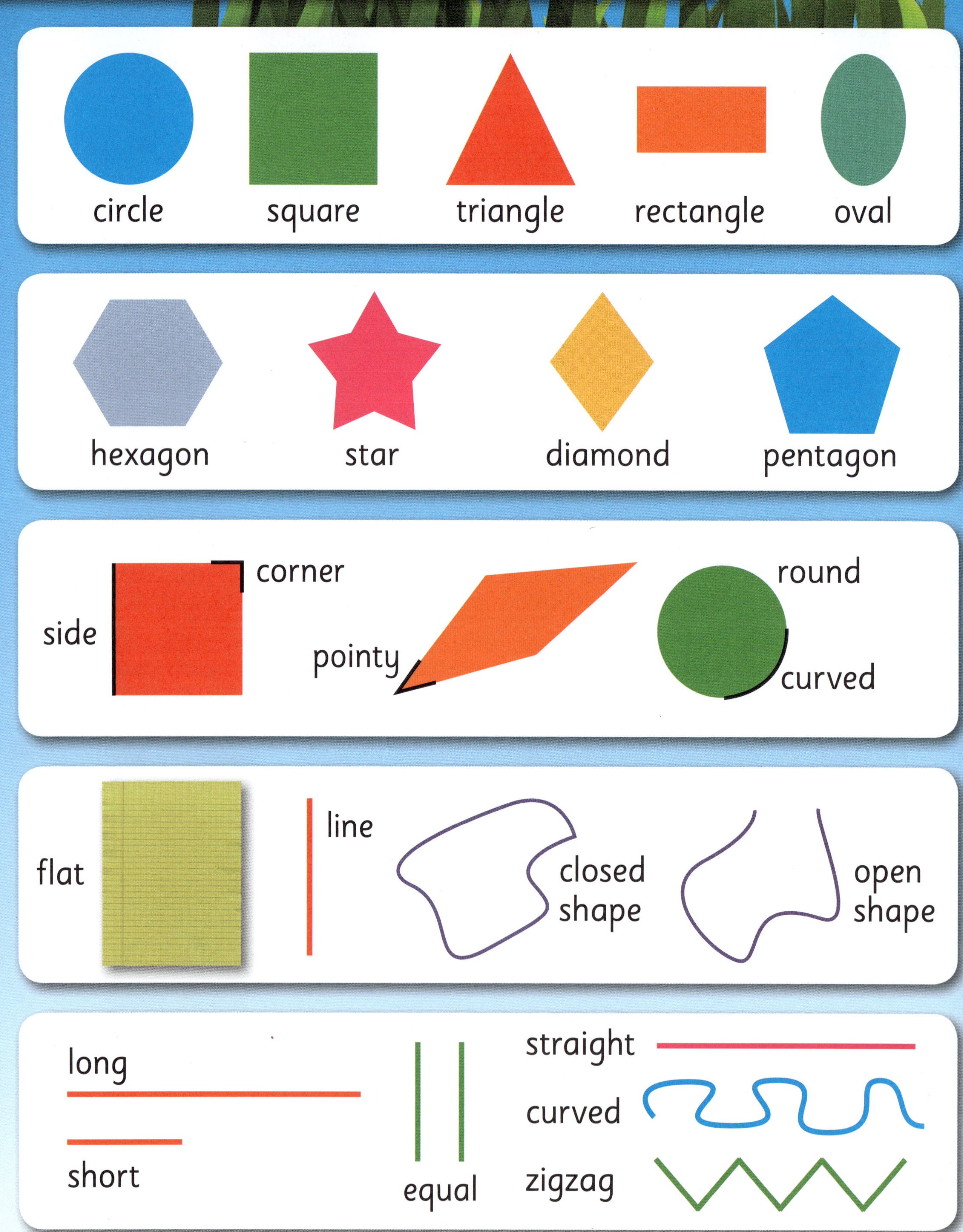

1 Match.

square | circle | triangle | rectangle

BUCKLE UP

2 Colour circles red, triangles green, rectangles yellow and squares blue.

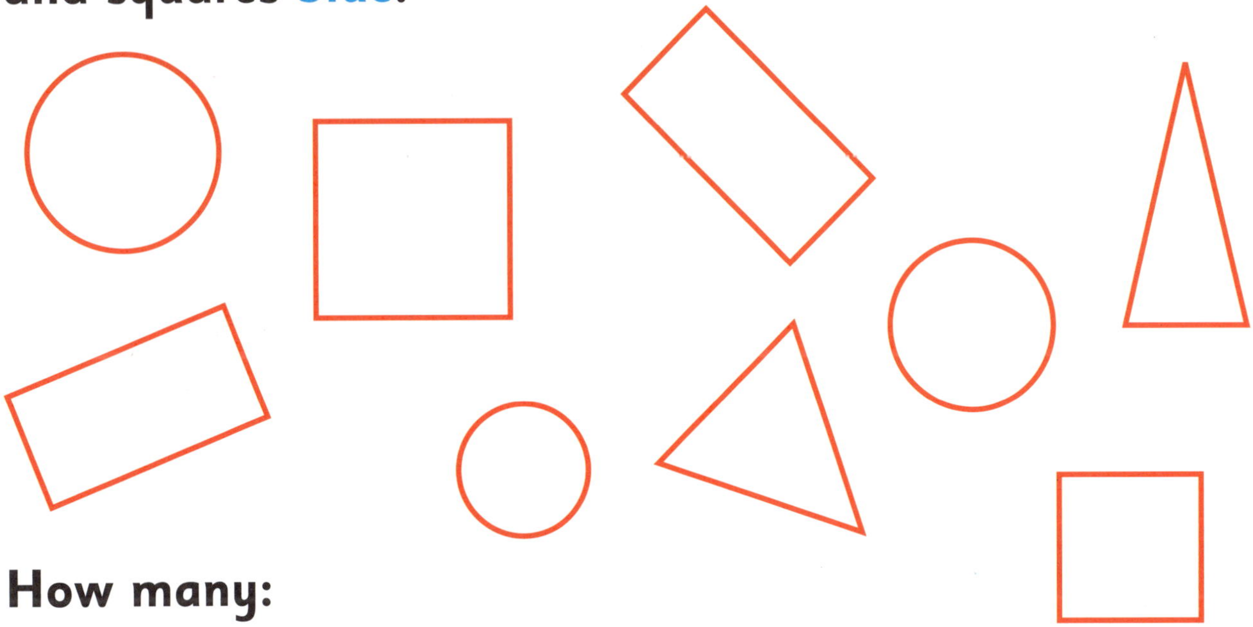

How many:

squares? ______ rectangles? ______

circles? ______ triangles? ______

3 Match.

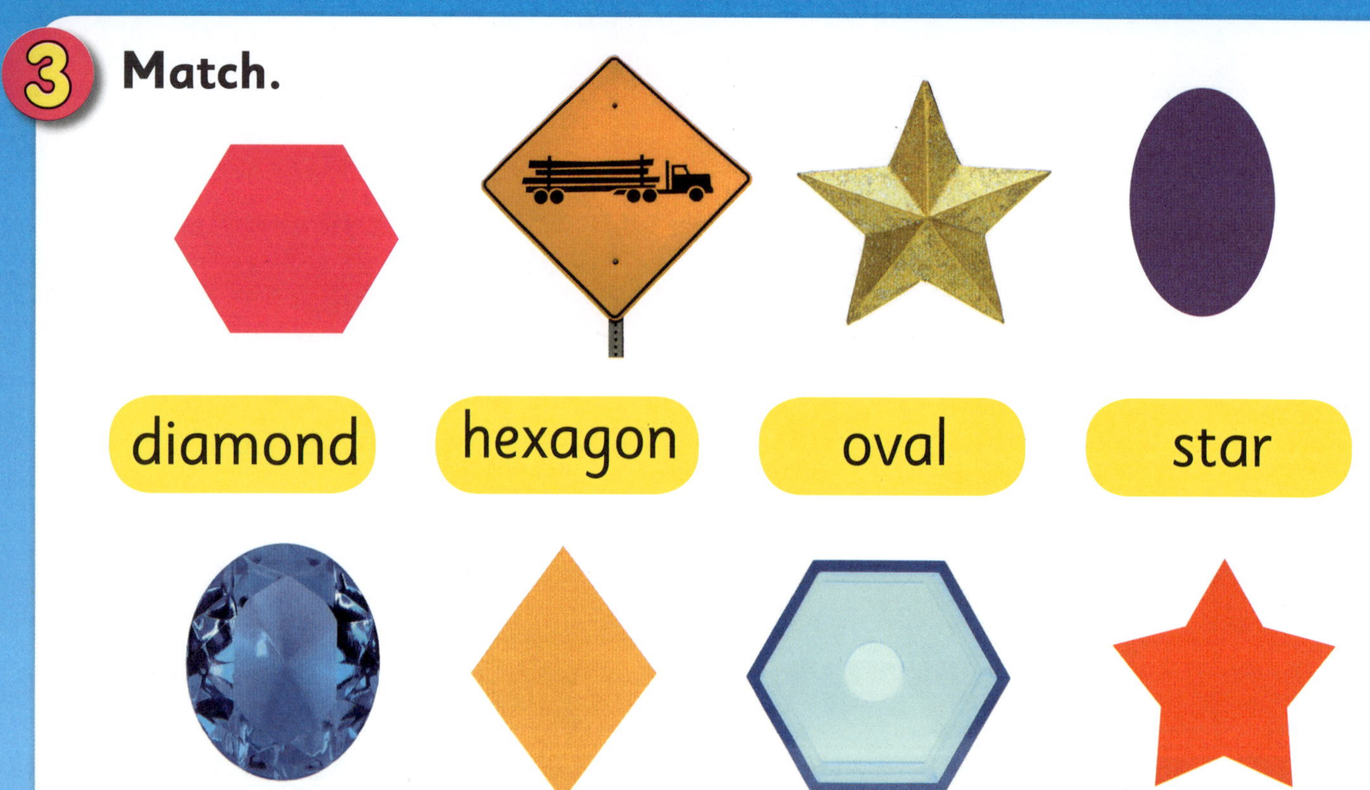

4 Read the clue and write the word.

I have 3 straight sides. I am a ________.	I am shaped like an egg. I am an ________.
I am round. I am a ________.	I have 6 straight sides. I am a ________.

5 Circle the shape words.

A circle is round. A square has four straight sides. All four sides are the same length. It has four corners.

Colour a shape each time you find a shape word.

6 Find something that is this shape. Draw it here.

circle	square
rectangle	triangle

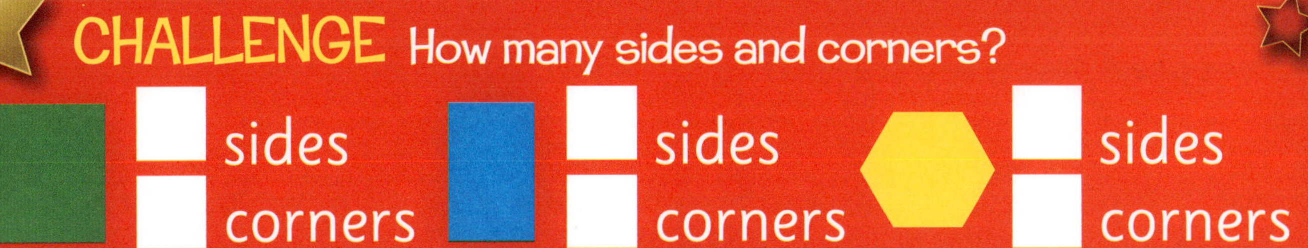

Unit 3 • At home

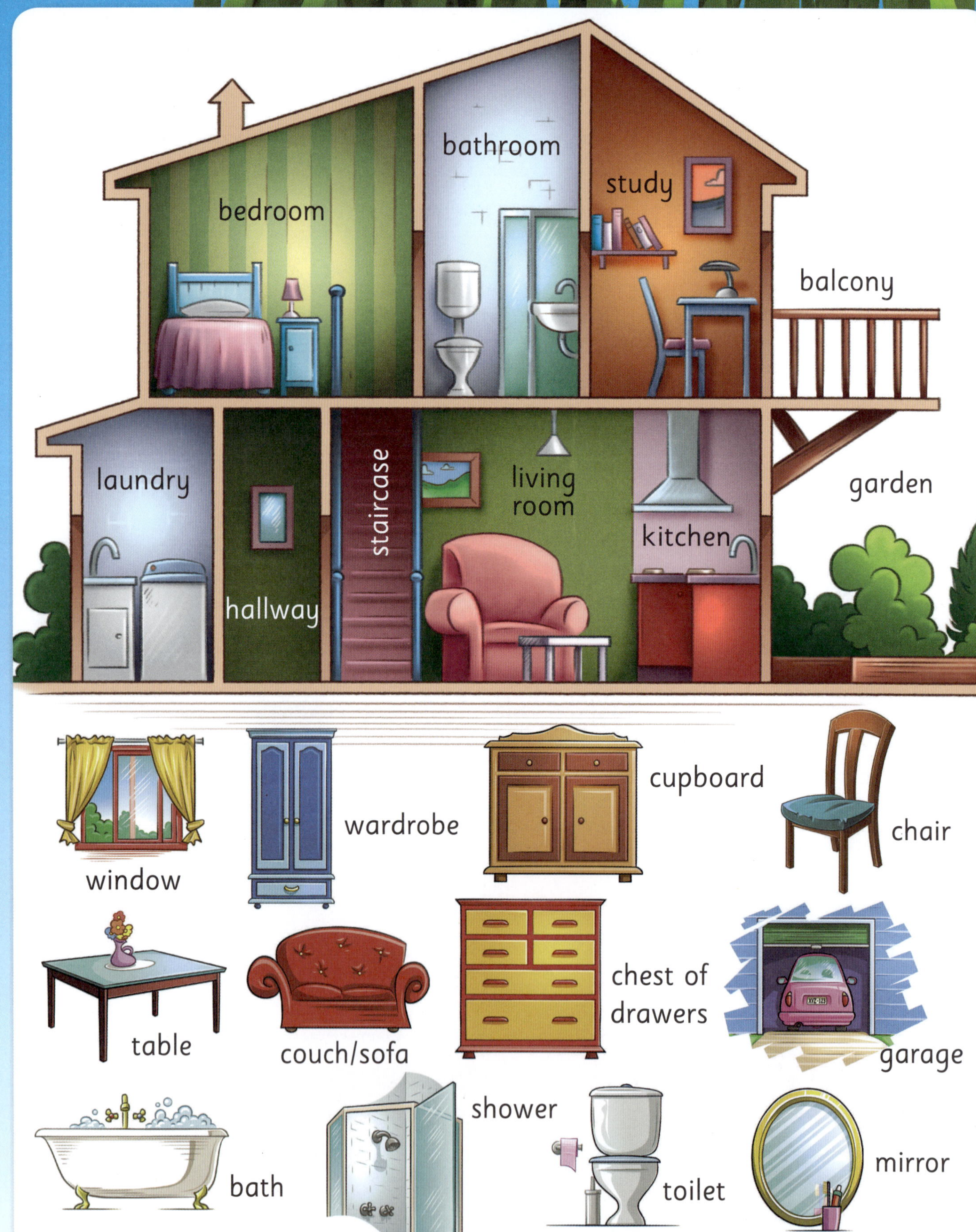

1 Match.

chair

table

window

bath

door

2 What goes where? Join each thing to a word.

teddy bear

bed

bookshelf

bedroom

toilet

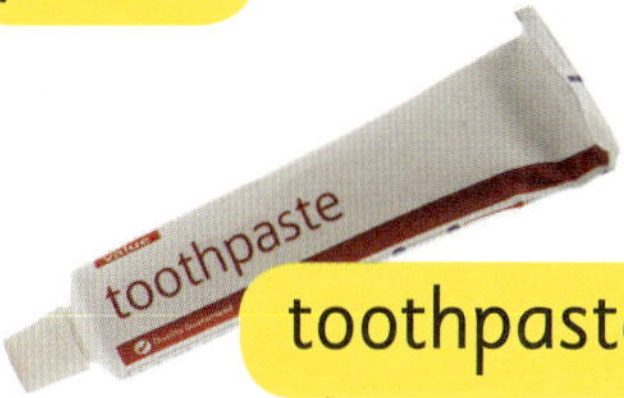

bathroom

toothbrush

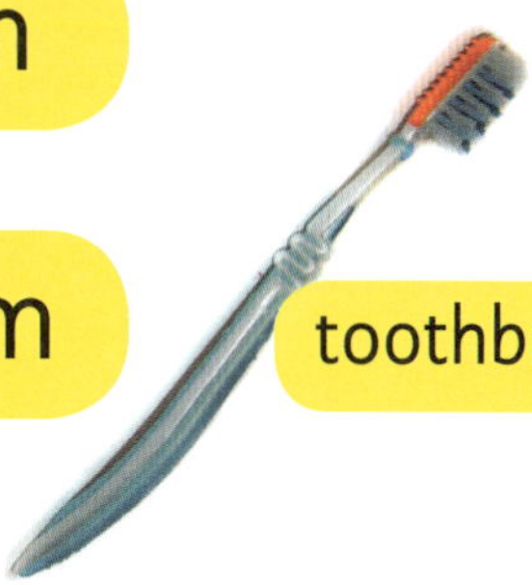

pillows

rug

toothpaste

towels

3 Read the clue and write the word.

One person can sit on me. I am a ______________.

You can see yourself in me. I am a ______________.

You sleep in this room. I am a ______________.

You put books here. I am a ______________.

4 Label each room. Use these words, living room, bathroom, kitchen, laundry.

5 Draw your bedroom here. Label your **bed**, **window** and **door**. Add other labels too.

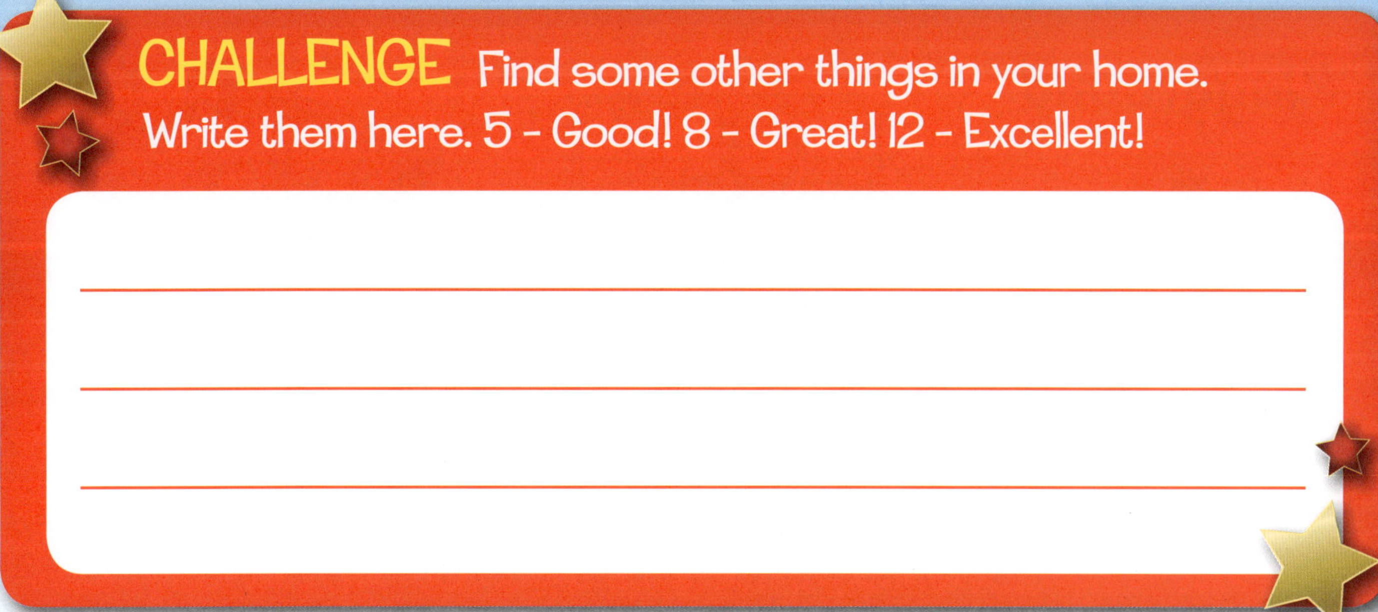

Unit 4 • Playtime

Inside toys

blocks

doll's house

teddy bear

bubbles

truck

playing cards

computer game

colouring book

board game

Outside sports and games

bicycle

tricycle

skipping rope

skateboard

football

basketball

Playground

roundabout

sandpit

climbing frame

slide

1 Match each word to a picture.

- blocks
- bubbles
- board game
- bicycle
- basketball
- skateboard

2 Label each picture.

3 **Join each picture to a word.**

4 **Choose the best word to complete each sentence.**

climbing frame roundabout slide sandpit

I climbed to the top of the ________________

________________.

I played with sand in the ________________.

I got dizzy on the ________________.

I slid down the slippery ________________.

5 **There is something missing in each picture. Read and draw the missing thing.**

 skateboard	 colouring book	 skipping rope
 bubbles	 slide	 bicycle

CHALLENGE

How many different ball games can you name?
4 - Good! 6 - Great! 8 - Excellent!

In the picture 1

Find the homewares.

Bathroom
- bath ✓
- towel
- shower
- toilet
- hand basin
- toothbrush
- mirror
- shampoo

Living room
- couch
- rug
- TV
- telephone
- vacuum cleaner

Kitchen
- table
- oven
- fridge
- toaster
- sink
- chair

Bedroom
- bed
- pillow
- bookcase
- window
- toys
- lamp

Unit 5 • Down on the farm

1 Match.

rooster

horse

sheep

goat

hen

cow

2 Join each animal to its home.

duck

sheep

pig

horse

paddock/field

pigsty

pond

stable

3 Draw.

a farmer on the tractor

a horse in the stable.

4 Is the sentence true or false? Circle one.

Cattle eat grass and hay. true or false

A scarecrow can dance and sing. true or false

A dam holds water. true or false

Milk comes from dairy cows. true or false

Roosters lay eggs. true or false

5 **Choose the best word to complete each sentence.**

cattle barn orchard farmhouse

The farmer lives in a ____________.

Dairy cows and other cows are called ____________.

Fruit trees grow in the ____________.

Hay is kept in the ____________.

CHALLENGE

Farmers grow many different crops for us to eat.
How many can you name? 4 - Good! 6 - Great! 8 - Excellent!

Unit 6 • At the shops

Chemist Newsagent Greengrocer Bakery Butcher

Department store Escalators Supermarket

Inside the supermarket

basket shelf

trolley customer assistant

coins register money wallet purse

1 Match.

shelf

credit card

register

escalator

greengrocer

2 Label each picture.

3 Match each picture to the shop that sells it.

4 **Read the clue and write the word.**

You can buy things with me. I am m______________.	I am a shop that sells meat. I am a b______________.
I sell all kinds of food. Shelves and shelves of it. I am a s______________.	You can buy dresses, perfume, toys and TV's here. I am a d______________.

5 **Label each part of the department store. Use these words, toys, clothes, electricals, furniture.**

CHALLENGE

How many other kinds of shops can you name?
3 - Good! 5 - Great! 7 - Excellent!

Unit 7 • 3D objects

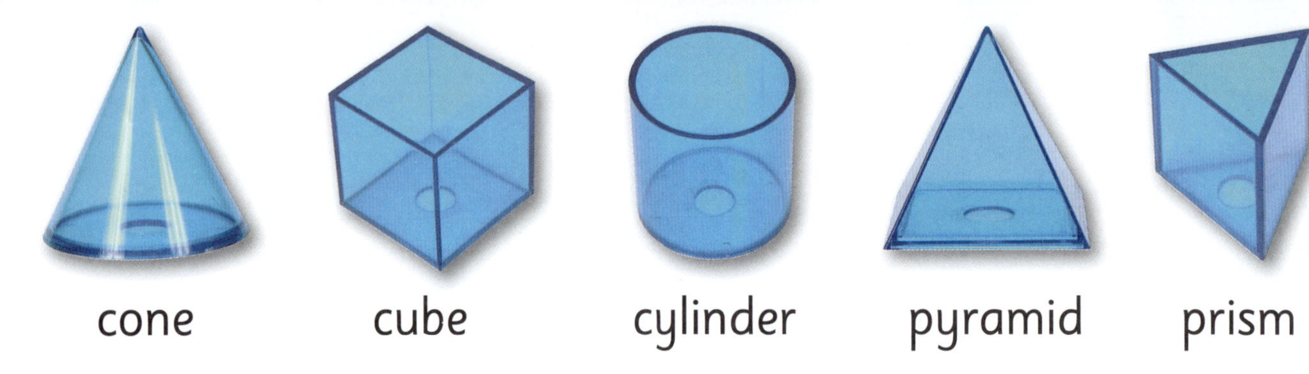

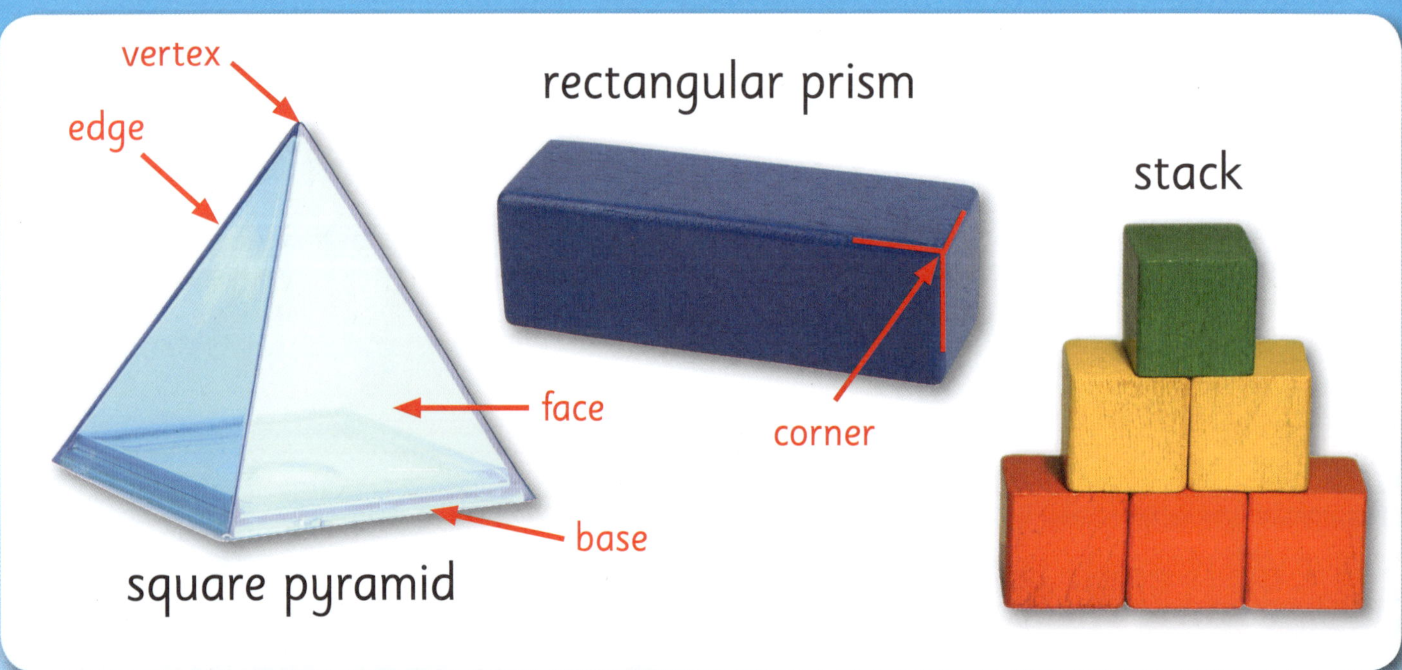

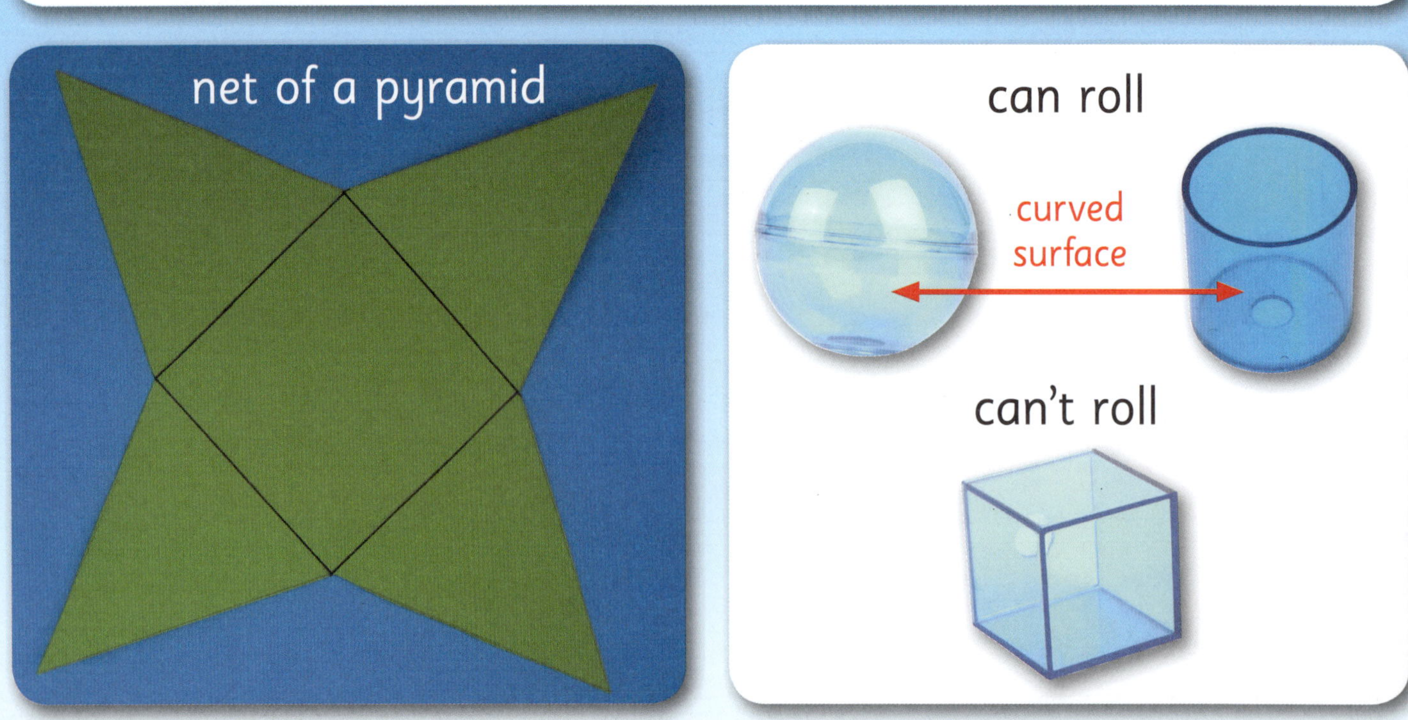

1 Match.

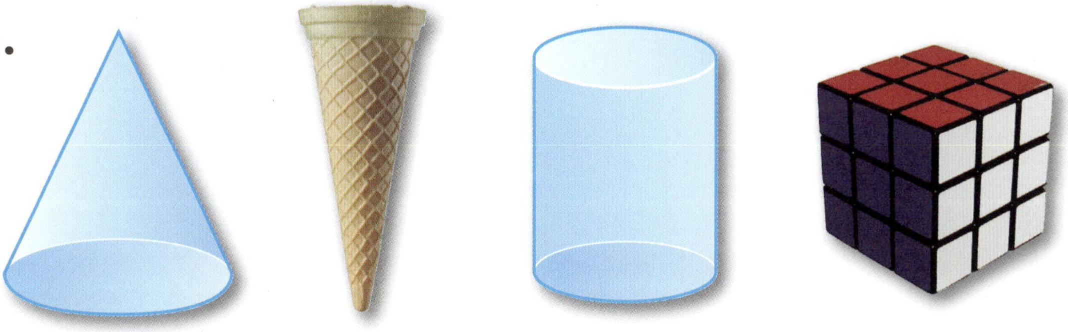

cone | cube | cylinder | pyramid

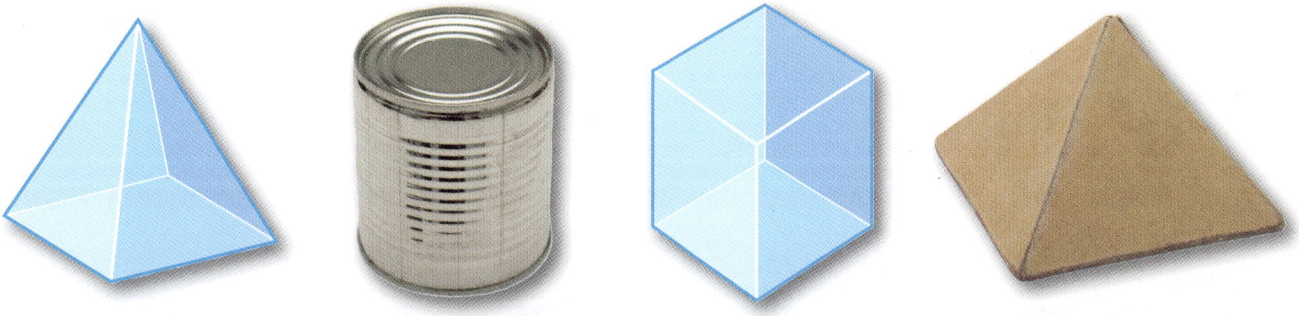

2 Colour cubes red, cylinders green, pyramids yellow and cones blue.

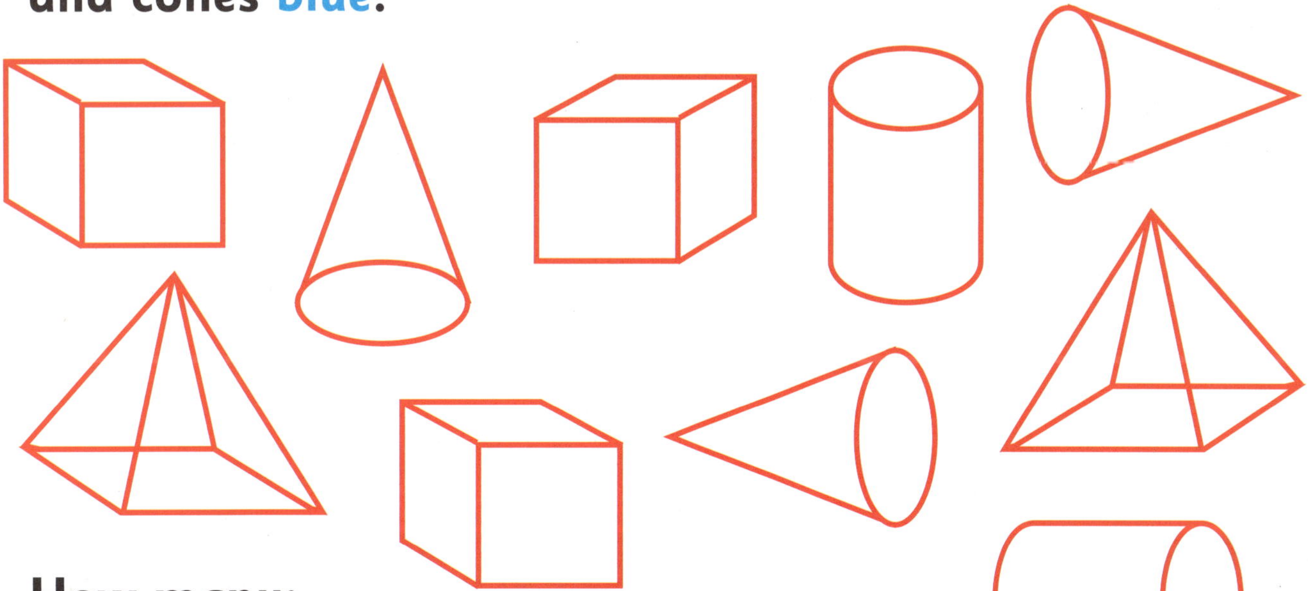

How many:

cubes? _____ cylinders? _____

pyramids? _____ cones? _____

3 **Match.**

sphere

triangular prism

rectangular prism

pyramid

4 **Read the clue and write the word.**

I am round like a ball. I am a s_________________.	I have 6 square sides. I am a __________________.
My 4 sides are triangles. My base is a square. I am a __________________.	I can roll. I can stack. My ends are circles. I am a __________________.

5 How many faces?

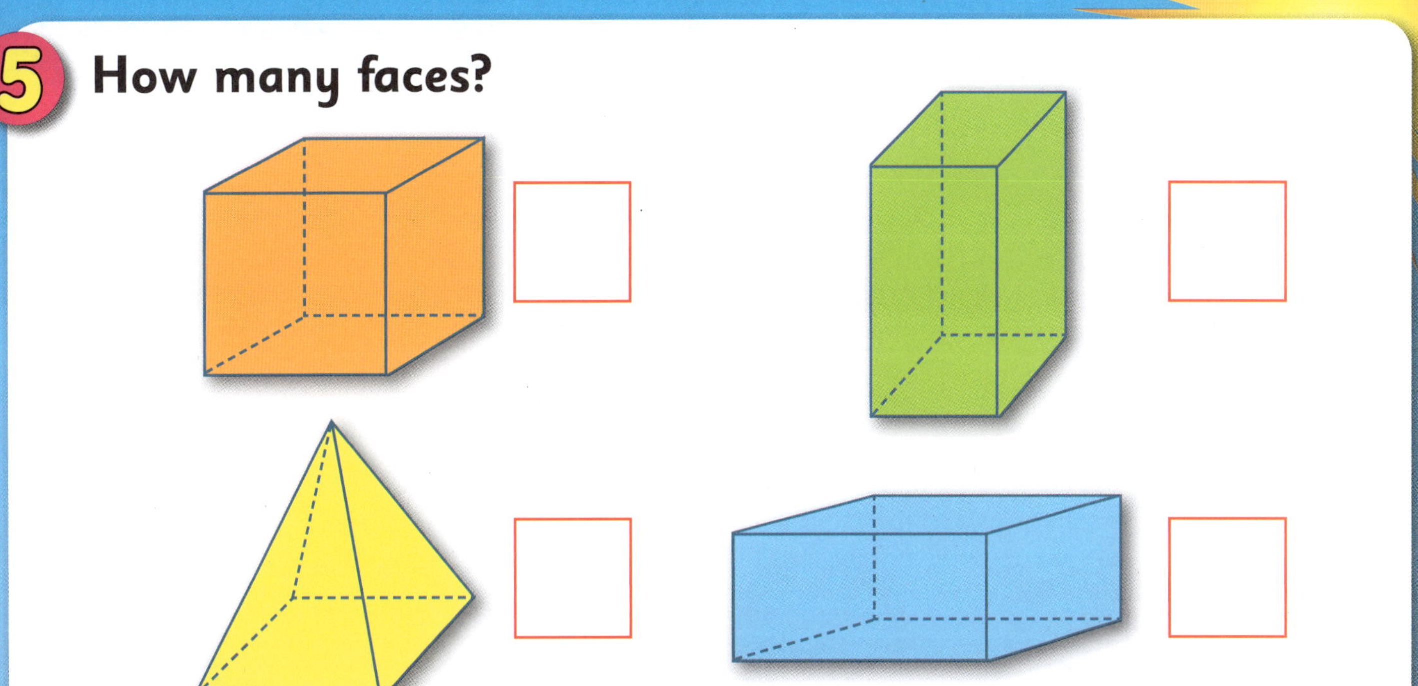

6 Find something that is this shape. Draw it here.

cube	cone
sphere	cylinder

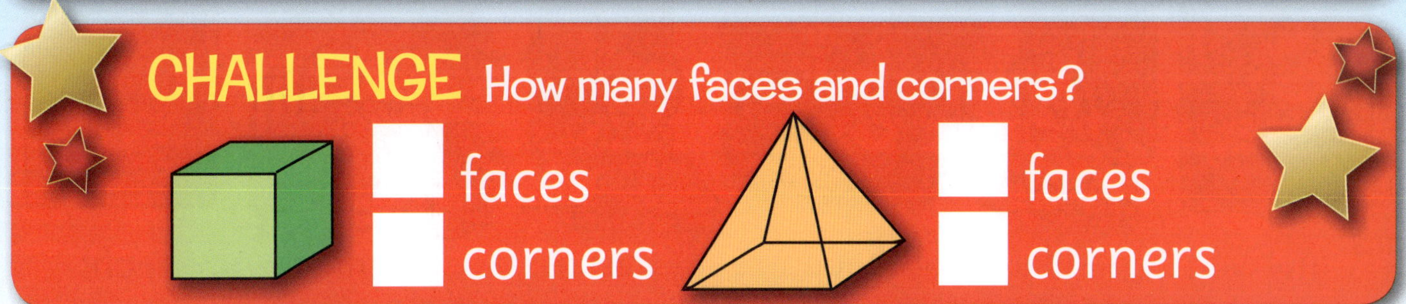

Unit 8 • Tick tock

analog

digital

3 o'clock

minute hand

hour hand

half past 3

quarter past 3

quarter to 3

The calendar

Days

Monday
Tuesday
Wednesday
Thursday
Friday
Saturday
Sunday

Months

January	July
February	August
March	September
April	October
May	November
June	December

Year

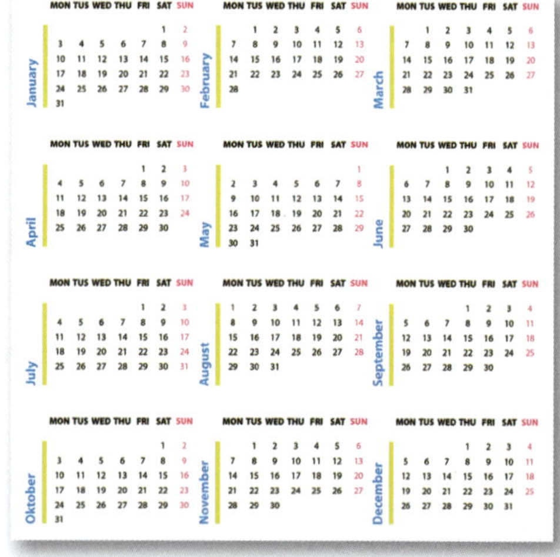

Daytime

morning

midday

afternoon

Night-time

evening

night

midnight

1 Join the word to its picture.

digital

minute hand

clock

quarter to 8

hour hand

watch

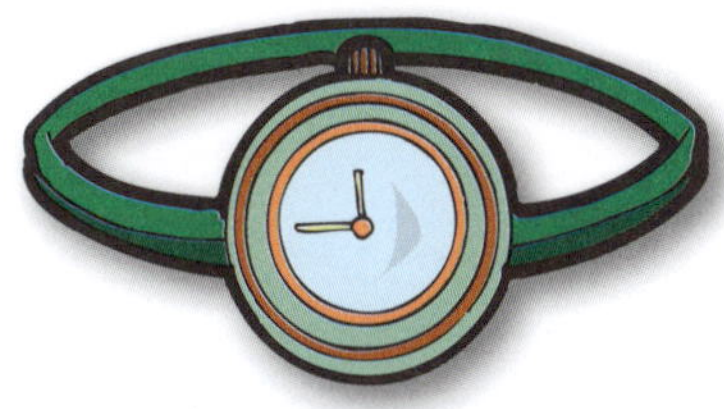

2 Draw.

an analog clock	a digital watch

Use this calendar to answer the questions.

Monday	Tuesday	Wednesday

Thursday	Friday	Saturday	Sunday

On which day did this happen?

 ____________________

 ____________________

 ____________________

 ____________________

 ____________________

 ____________________

 ____________________

4 Complete.

January	July
February	August
M__________	S__________
April	October
May	November
J__________	D__________

5 Choose the best word to complete each sentence.

evening midday morning night

I eat breakfast in the ____________.

The moon and stars come out at ____________.

The sun begins to set in the ____________.

I eat my lunch at ____________.

CHALLENGE

Find the dates of 5 people's birthdays.
Use a calendar to help you write the dates in order.

In the picture 2

Fruit and vegetables
- bananas
- broccoli
- watermelon
- cauliflower

Meat and fish
- sausages
- chicken
- salmon

Frozen
- ice-cream
- pizza
- burgers

Chilled
- yoghurt
- cheese
- butter

Tins
- baked beans
- soup
- tuna

Pasta and rice
- spaghetti
- couscous
- brown rice

Personal
- toothpaste
- shampoo
- tissues

Find the grocery items.

Unit 9 • Party time

Party things

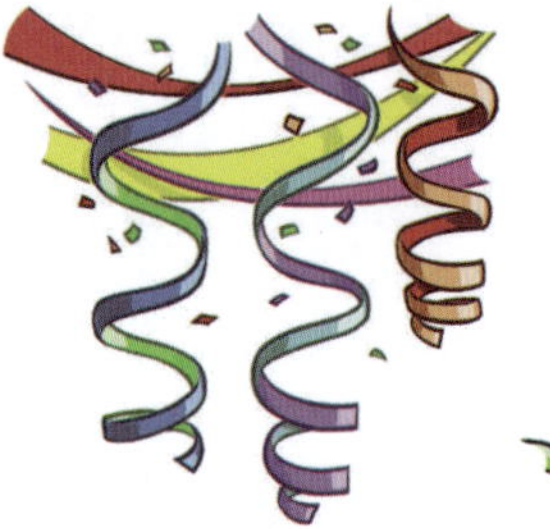

streamers

balloon

popper

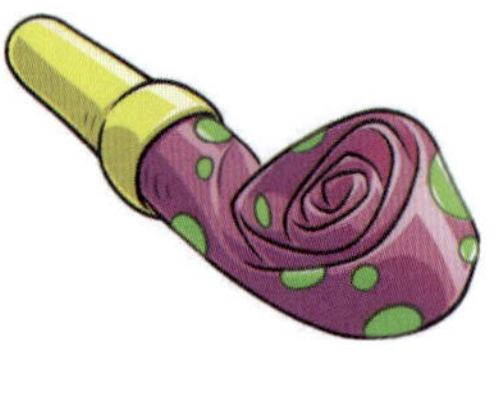

blower

candles

present

card

music

game

costume

Party food

cake

jelly

ice-cream

lollies

Party people

magician

fairy

clown

guest

1 Match.

- candles
- fairy
- card
- jelly
- popper

2 Draw:

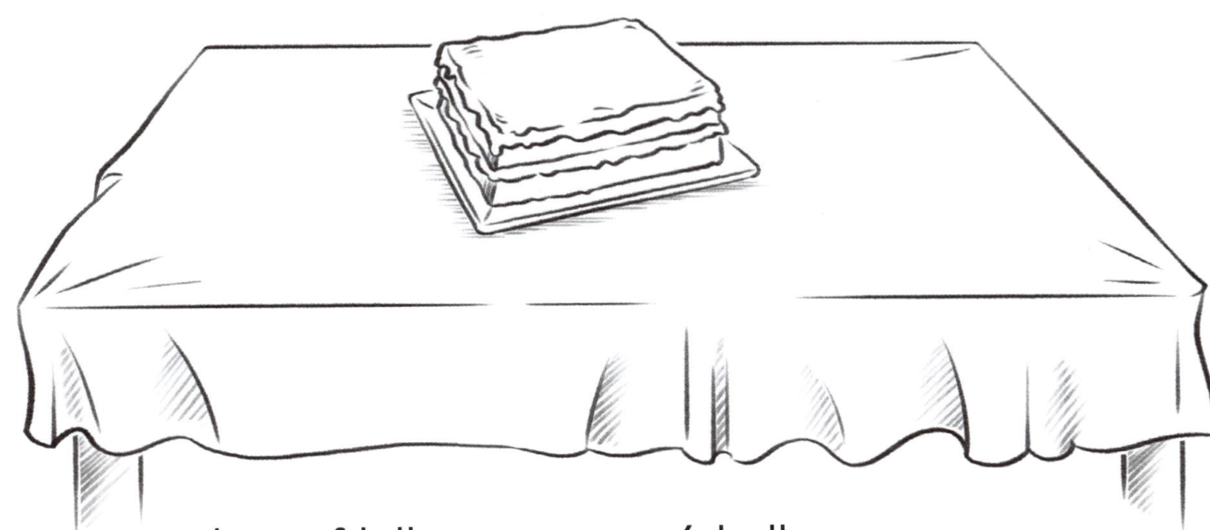

- a plate of lollies.
- red streamers.
- 4 balloons.
- 6 candles on the cake.

3 Join the object to the person.

4 Colour the party things red. Colour the party food blue.

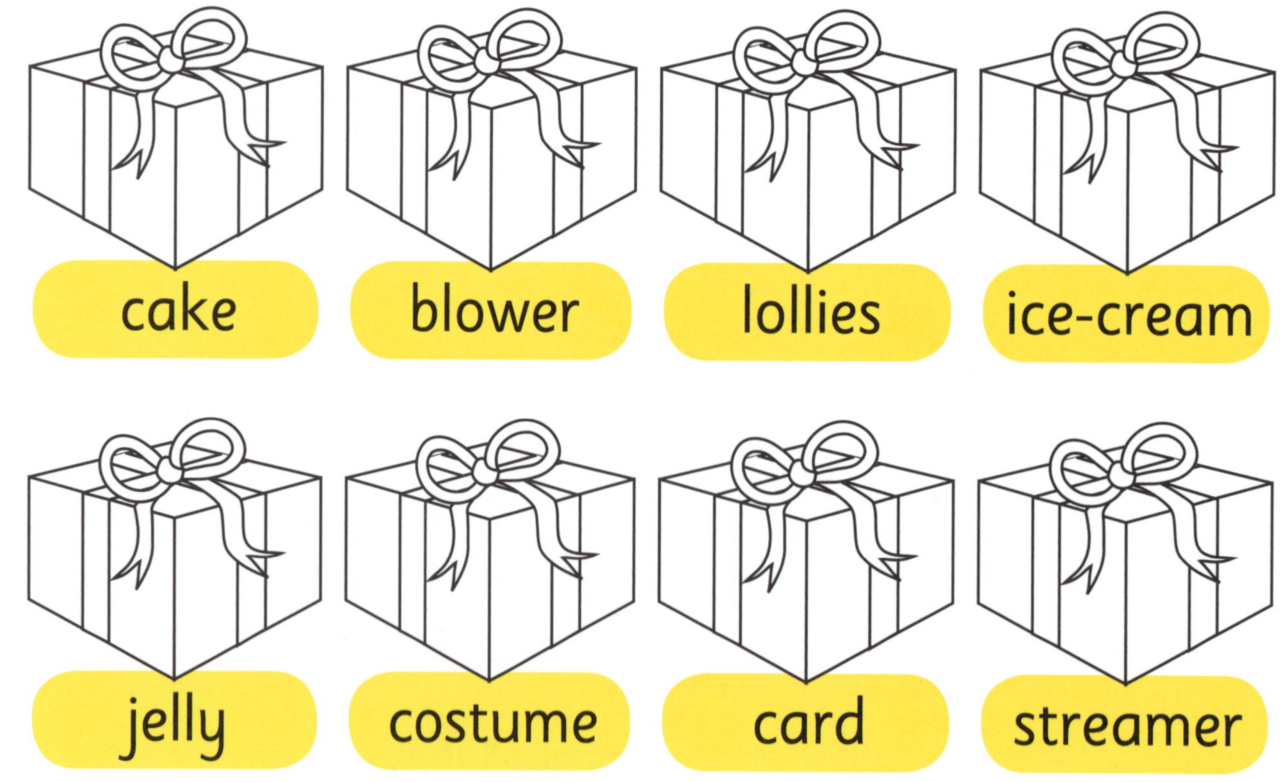

5 **Help Meg find her birthday cake. Draw a track of party words.**

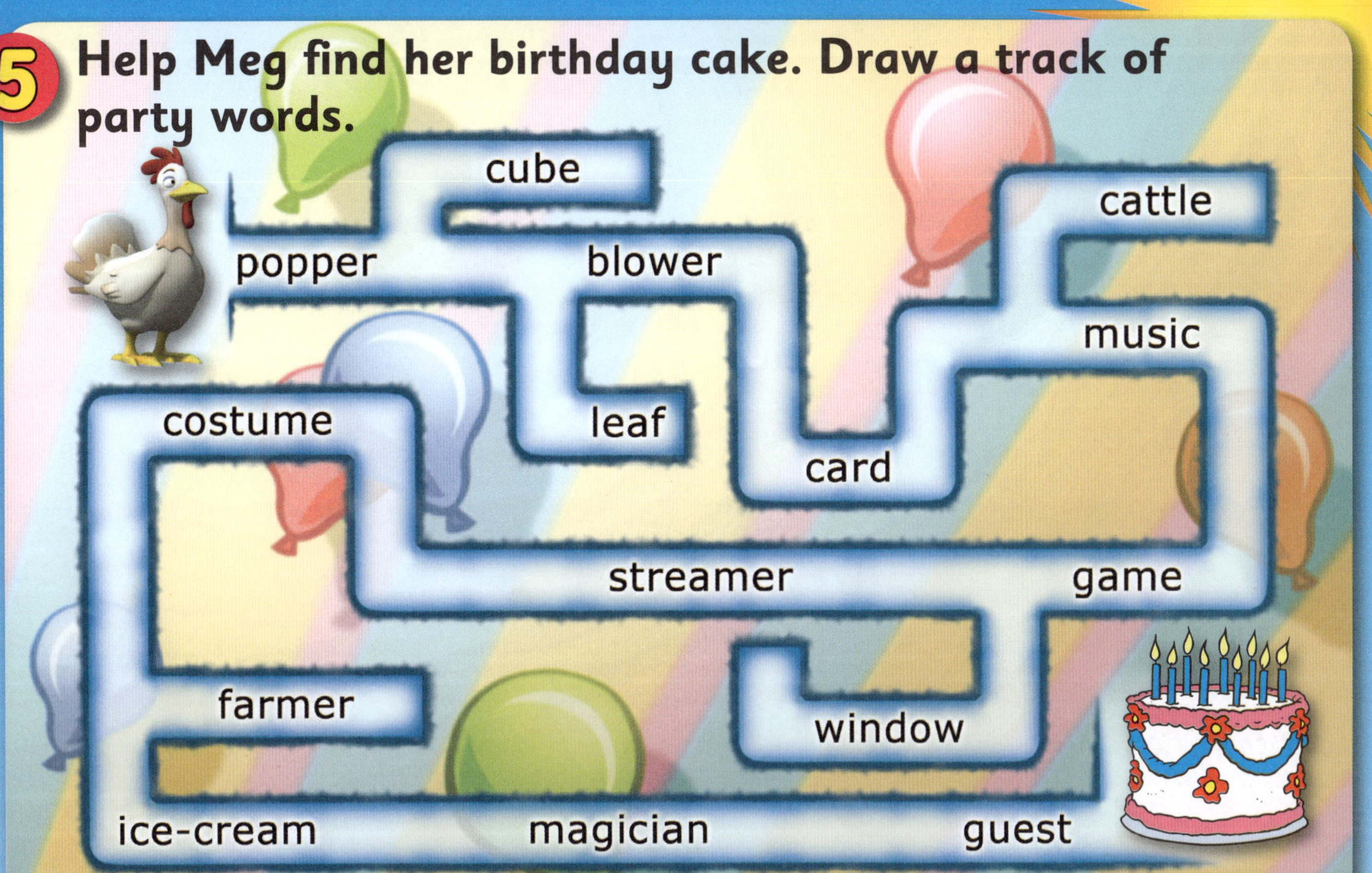

6 **Circle the correct word. Cross out the wrong word.**

The music magician did tricks at my party.

I wore a superhero clown costume .

The party poppers candles made a loud BANG!

Everyone danced to the blower music .

CHALLENGE Plan a birthday party. Make a list of:

- party games
- party food
- guests

Unit 10 • Moving around

Air

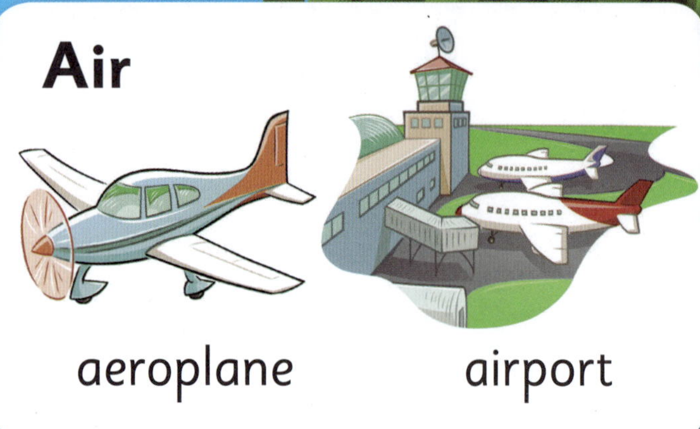

aeroplane airport

Sea

ferry cruise ship port

Land

bicycle motorbike 4-wheel drive taxi motorway

train railway station tram wharf monorail

People

Don't forget!

passenger driver pilot captain

ticket passport luggage

1 Match each word to a picture.

ferry

monorail

luggage

driver

taxi

motorbike

2 Where do I catch ... ? Join the transport to the place.

train

cruise ship

aeroplane

ferry

port

airport

wharf

station

3 Complete the labels.

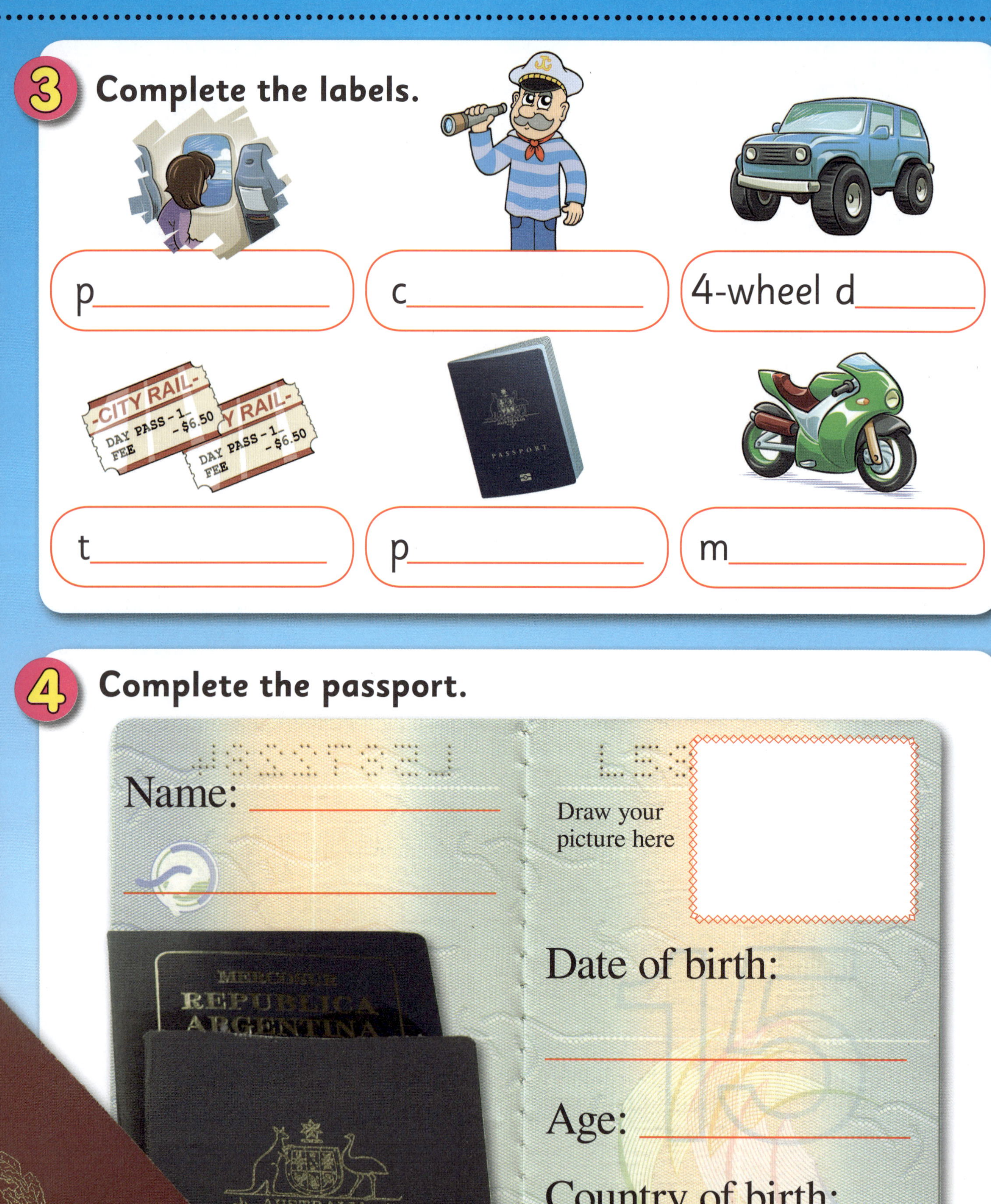

p__________

c__________

4-wheel d__________

t__________

p__________

m__________

4 Complete the passport.

Name: __________

____

Draw your picture here

Date of birth:

____

Age: __________

Country of birth:

____

5 Read the clue and write the word.

I run on a single rail. I am a ______________.	You can pack your clothes in me. I am ______________.
You can catch a train from here. I am a ______________.	I have powerful engines to make me fly. I am an ______________.

6 Is the sentence true or false? Circle one.

A ferry travels in the air.	true or false
Cars can travel on a motorway.	true or false
A pilot flies an aeroplane.	true or false
A bicycle sails across the sea.	true or false

CHALLENGE How many different things can you think of that move around on wheels?
4 - Good! 6 - Great! 8 - Excellent!

Unit 11 • Ahoy me hearties!

Pirate

captain's hat

eye patch

cutlass

parrot

scarf

scar

map

earring

knife

boots

treasure

Pirate ship

sails

flag

cannon

lookout

deck

shipwreck

rigging

plank

Ahoy me hearties?

1 Match.

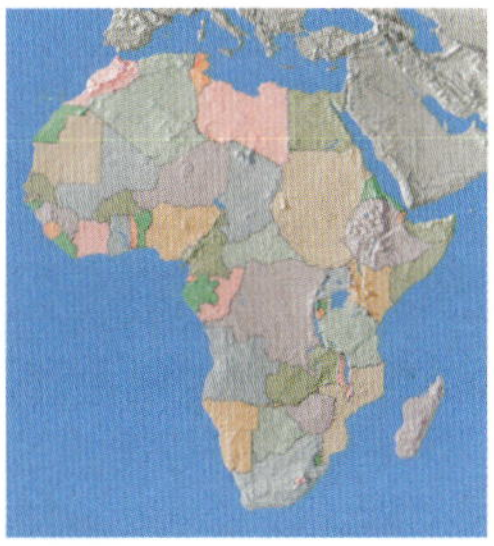

treasure

parrot

knife

map

2 Label the pirate ship.

f__________

l__________

s__________

r__________

d__________

c__________

p__________

3 Colour the word if it belongs to a pirate.

4 Help the pirate find the treasure. Colour the path of the pirate ship words.

sails	cannon	tree	shell	fish
sand	lookout	deck	hole	leaf
plant	sun	rigging	bird	crab
rock	cave	shipwreck	plank	

Ahoy me hearties?

5 **Circle the pirate words.**

The pirate stood on the deck. He wore an earring and big, black boots. He and his parrot were looking for treasure.

Colour in a flag each time you find a word.

6 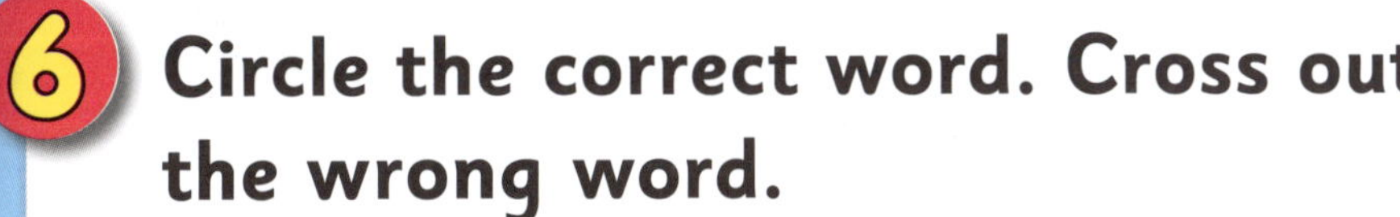

Circle the correct word. Cross out the wrong word.

This is a pirate mermaid .

Pirates have to climb the mountain rigging .

This pirate had to walk the plank street .

Here is a shipwreck playground .

CHALLENGE Write these words in alphabetical order:

sails deck knife boots flag

Unit 12 • People who help us

Help me stay healthy

doctor

nurse

dentist

pharmacist

Help me to be safe

police officer

firefighter

paramedic

Help me fix things

builder

carpenter

electrician

mechanic

plumber

Help me learn

teacher

librarian

principal

parents

Help my community

postal worker

garbage collector

gardener

ranger

1 Draw a line from the person to the word.

doctor   builder   teacher

firefighter   gardener

2 What do I use? Match.

nurse

carpenter

librarian

police officer

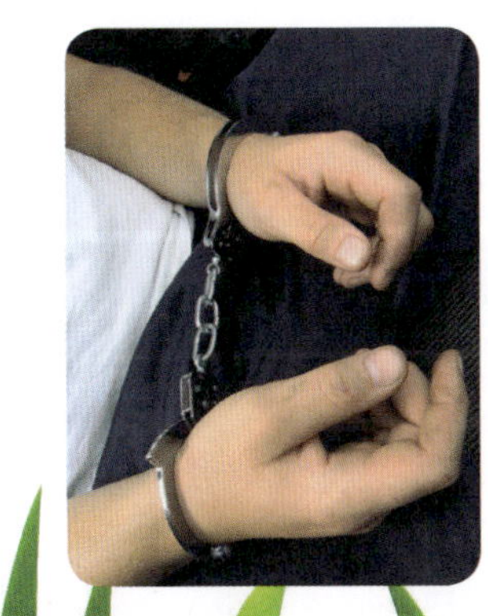

postal worker

3 Who do I need to call ...

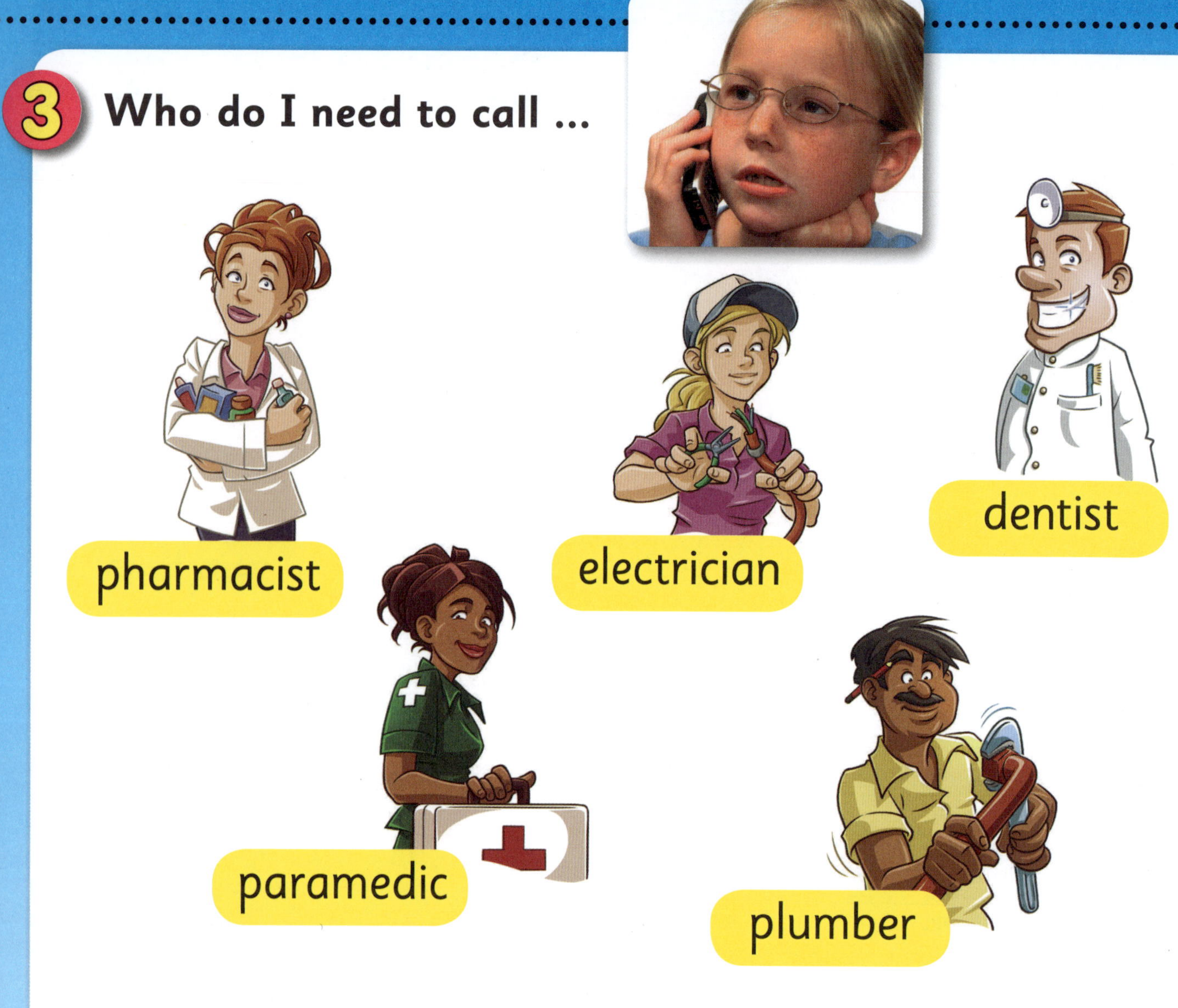

to fix my leaking tap? ______________________________

to check my teeth? ______________________________

to take me to hospital? ______________________________

to fix a switch? ______________________________

to get my medicine? ______________________________

4 Who's missing? Draw and label the missing person.

b________________

f________________

5 Choose the best word to complete each sentence.

ranger principal mechanic parents

A ________________ fixes broken cars and engines.

My ________________ look after my sister and I.

The ________________ is in charge of a school.

A ________________ looks after parks and wildlife.

CHALLENGE Can you name any more people that help you and your family?
4 - Good! 6 - Great! 8 - Excellent!

In the picture 3

Find everything on this treasure island.

At sea

- dolphin
- mermaid
- turtle
- shipwreck
- pirate ship

On the beach

- sand
- shells
- starfish
- coral
- seaweed
- driftwood
- chest
- treasure
- bonfire
- map

In the forest

- palm tree
- coconuts
- waterfall
- lagoon
- rocks
- rockpool
- cave

Unit 13 • Ordinal numbers

1 Match.

9th	second	10th
	eighth	
2nd	fourth	8th
	tenth	
4th	sixth	6th
	ninth	

2 Join the critter to their medal.

3

CAT SHOW

Answer the questions.

Who came fifth? ____________________

Who came second? ____________________

Who came fourth? ____________________

Who came first? ____________________

Who came third? ____________________

4 **Colour:**

- the sixth bead **red**.
- the ninth bead **blue**.
- the eighth bead **yellow**.
- the tenth bead **green**.
- the seventh bead **orange**.

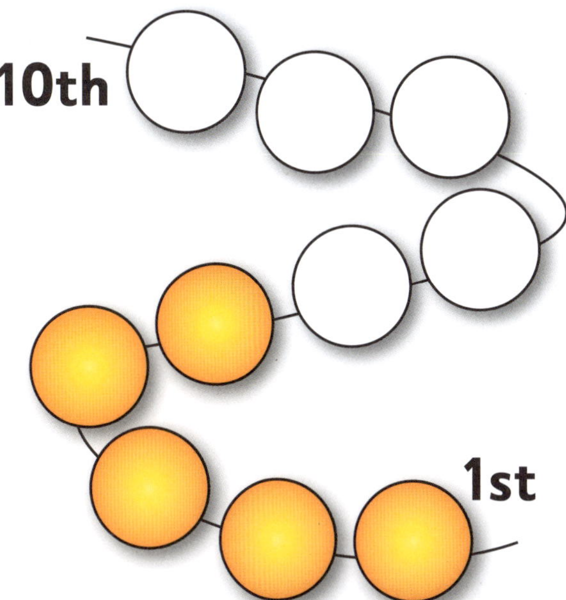

5 **Read the clue and write the word.**

Flobby came between sixth and eighth place. Flobby came ____________.	Yetiyo came between seventh and ninth place. Yetiyo came ____________.
Pinkipoo came between fifth and seventh place. Pinkipoo came ____________.	Happy Nap came between eighth and tenth place. Happy Nap came ____________.

CHALLENGE Find out what the ordinal number is for:

11 13 15 17 20

Unit 14 • At the restaurant

People

On the table

My order

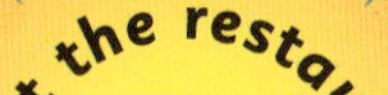

1 Match.

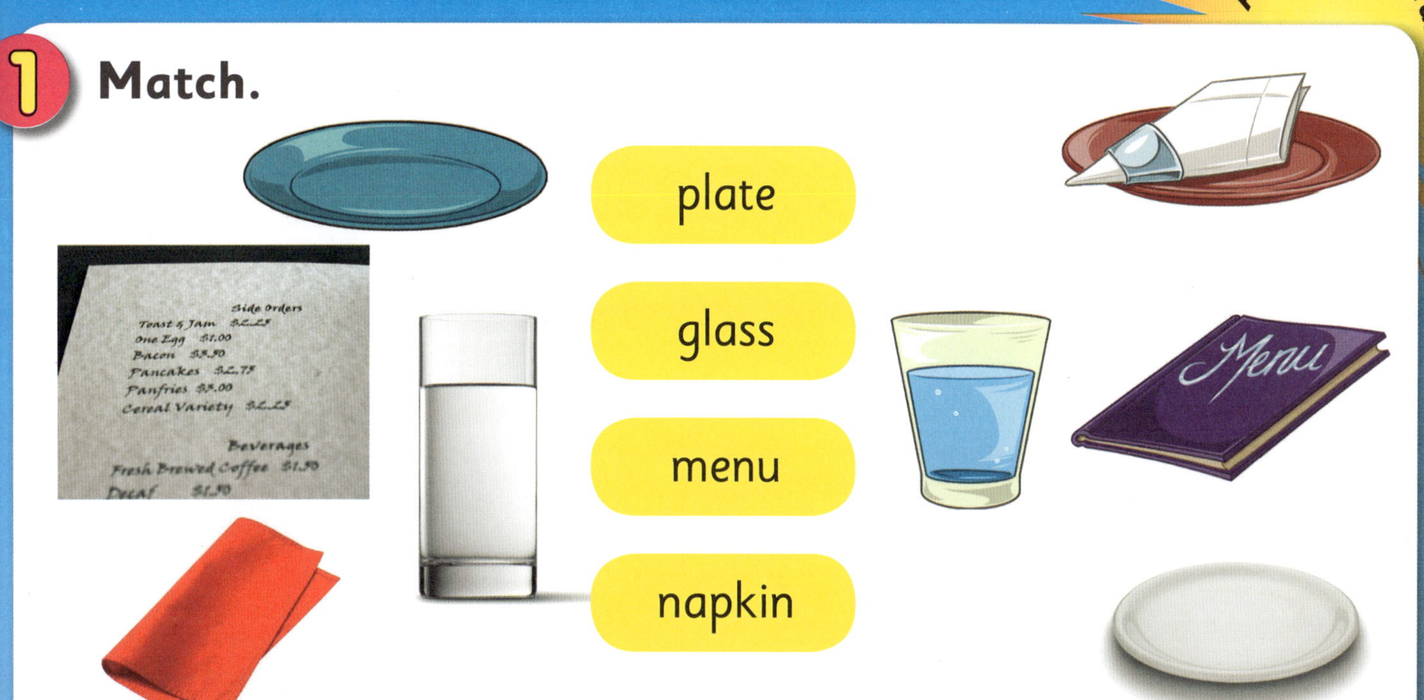

- plate
- glass
- menu
- napkin

2 Write the words in the correct place.

on the table

food

- knife
- lunch
- fork
- dinner
- salad
- spoon

3 Draw.

a yummy dessert

a big breakfast

4 Label the pictures. Use these words.

drink chef waiter chair

5 **Circle the restaurant words.**

The customer sat at the table and the waiter took her order. Her dessert was apple pie. When she was finished, she paid the bill and thanked the chef.

Colour in a plate each time you find a word.

6 **Circle the correct word. Cross out the wrong word.**

You eat soup with a knife spoon.

The first meal of the day is breakfast dinner.

Use a bill napkin to wipe your mouth.

The chef dentist cooks food at the restaurant.

CHALLENGE

Plan a restaurant menu. Decide what you will serve for:

starters dinner dessert drinks

Unit 15 • Seasonal things

Spring

lamb

daffodils

blossom

buds

nest

Summer

beach

sunscreen

sunglasses

umbrella

swimmers

Autumn

leaves

chestnuts

twigs

rain

rake

Winter

snowman

skiing

frost

fog

fireplace

1 Match.

lamb | beach | fog | rake | nest

2 Write the words in the correct place.

summer

swimmers | sunglasses | skiing

sunscreen | snowman | frost

3 Label each picture. Use these words.

spring   summer   autumn   winter

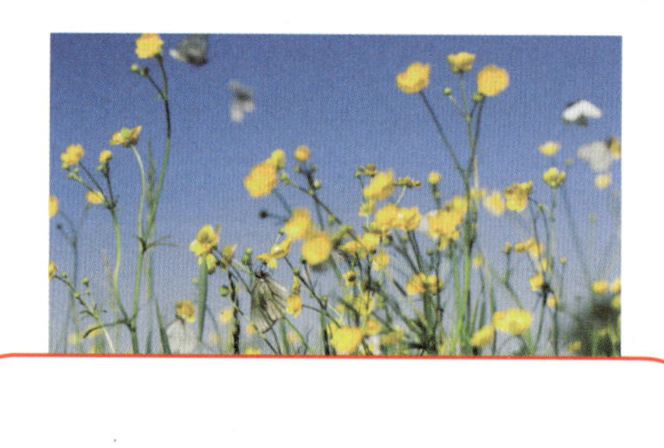

4 Colour the autumn words orange. Colour the spring words green.

daffodils

leaves

rake

blossoms

chestnuts

lamb

twigs

buds

5 **Read the clue to write the word.**

You can make a snowman during this season. It is ______________.

You need to wear your sunscreen during this season. It is ______________.

Little buds begin to blossom on trees during this season. It is ______________.

You will need to rake up lots of fallen leaves during this season. It is ______________.

6 **Circle the correct word. Cross out the wrong word.**

Sit by the blossoms fireplace to keep warm.

It is cool and shady under the umbrella buds.

The bird's nest twigs has three blue eggs.

I can't see the trees because of the rake fog.

CHALLENGE

Find out which months of the year are spring, summer, autumn, winter.

Unit 16 • Things to wear

Head

beanie

helmet

glasses

mask

headphones

Body

underwear

T-shirt

shirt

skirt

trousers

cardigan

jacket

overalls

wetsuit

life jacket

Feet

flippers

skis

rollerblades

ice skates

slippers

1 Match.

2 Join the words to the correct suitcase.

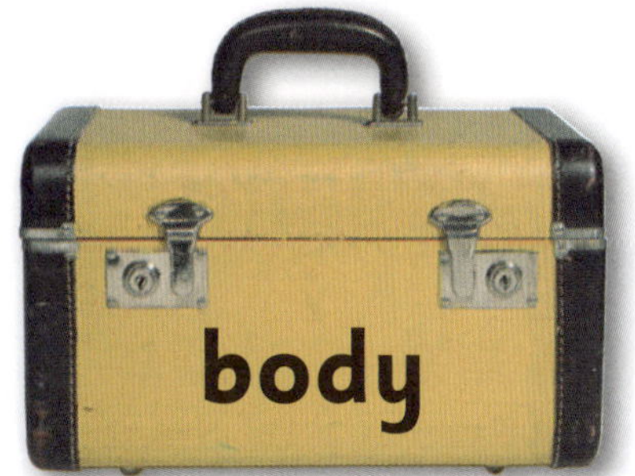

helmet jacket slippers skirt

glasses ice skates

3 Draw.

a mask and flippers on this diver

a helmet and rollerblades on this skater

4 Label the pictures. Use these words.

overalls wetsuit shirt skis

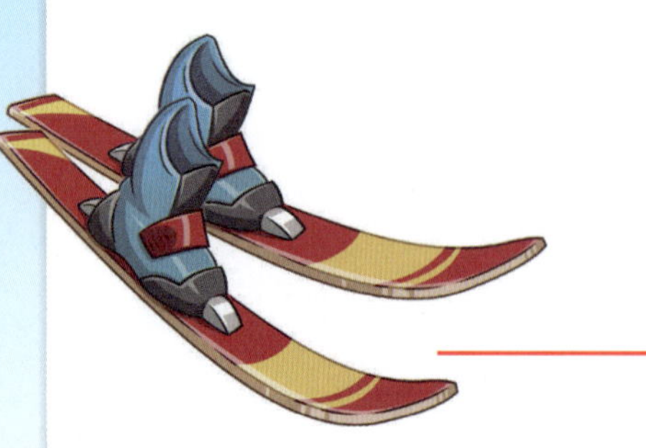

5 Circle the things to wear words.

I am going sailing. I put on my beanie to keep my head warm. I wear my T-shirt, trousers and a cardigan. Next I put on my warm jacket. Lastly I wear a life jacket to keep me safe.

Colour in a T-shirt each time you find a word.

6 Choose the best word to complete each sentence.

headphones overalls underwear wetsuit

He wears ______________ to keep his clothes clean.

I wear a ______________ when I surf.

Listen to music through your ______________.

I put on my ______________ first when I get dressed.

CHALLENGE How many more things can you wear on your feet? 4 - Good! 6 - Great! 8 - Excellent!

In the picture 4

CHEF

Revision

1 Match each word to its picture.

daughter

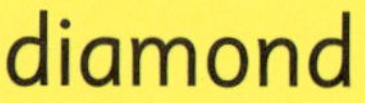
diamond

laundry

basketball

tractor

escalator

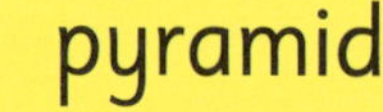
pyramid

digital

calendar

magician

monorail

treasure

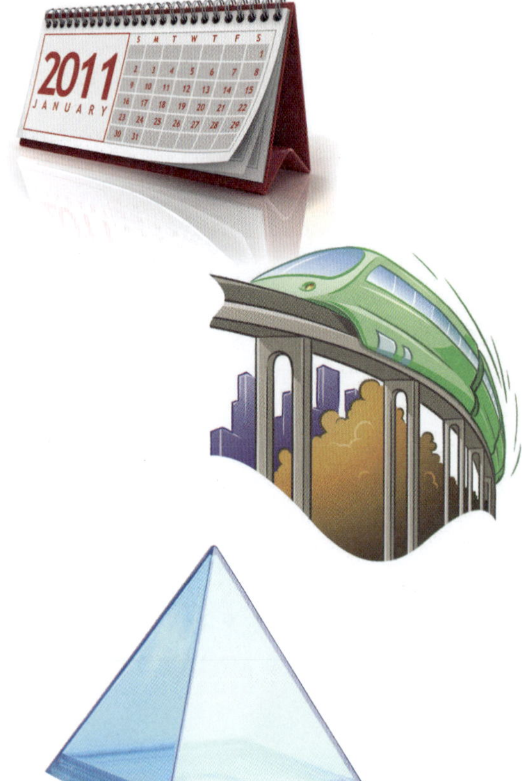

2 Write the words in the correct place.

menu	beanie	fourth	life jacket
frost	napkin	second	waiter
ninth	snowman	rollerblades	daffodils

ordinal numbers

restaurant

seasonal things

things to wear

GREAT WORK!
Your Vocabulary is excellent!